The Diversity,

Pı

Author: Quincy M. Wright, CCM, PMP

First published by PMO Nerd LLC

The Diversity, Equity, and Inclusion Mindset in Project Management

Copyright 2022 by PMO Nerd LLC. All rights reserved.

Our copyright content is protected by U.S. intellectual property law that is recognized by most countries. No part of this publication may be reproduced, stored, or transmitted in any form or by any means, electronic, manual, mechanical, photocopying, recording, scanning, or otherwise, without written permission from the publisher. It is illegal to copy this book, post it to a website, or distribute it by any other means without permission.

First Edition

ISBN: 979-8-218-00679-2 (Paper Book)
ISBN: 979-8-218-01610-4 (eBook)

Published by:
PMO Nerd LLC
Email: Support@pmonerd.com
Web: www.pmonerd.com

Dedication

To My Family and Friends:

The first edition of this book would not have happened without my family and friends' help, support, encouragement, and valuable feedback. A book like this takes a village, and I want to thank my village.

To Project Managers:

My goal is to provide a roadmap to help project managers foster an equitable project team environment without barriers to opportunities, including developing an inclusive space where all team members feel welcomed, valued, respected, and engaged.

Table of Contents

Acknowledgement	*I*
Introduction	*II*
The Science and Art of Project Management	*1*
Fundamentals of Diversity, Equity, and Inclusion	*27*
Social Identity Influence in Project Management	*39*
Creating a Winning Team	*57*
Leading a Winning Team	*77*
Improving Team Performance	*89*
Inclusive Leadership	*101*
Developing a Growth Mindset in Leadership	*111*
About the Author	*122*
About PMO Nerd LLC	*123*

Acknowledgement

I would like to recognize Woodrow Winchester, III, PhD, CPEM, for his support, encouragement, and input on The Diversity, Equity, and Inclusion Mindset in Project Management.

Woodrow W. Winchester, III, PhD, CPEM, is currently the Executive Director of Texas Engineering Executive Education (TxEEE) at The University of Texas at Austin. Woodrow is a Certified Professional Engineering Management Professional (CPEMÒ) with over ten (10) years of technical program and project management experience. Woodrow is also the inaugural Director of Diversity, Equity, and Inclusion (DE/I) for the American Society for Engineering Management (ASEM). Selected as a member of the second cohort of the NSF-sponsored IAspire Leadership Academy, Woodrow is a champion for more equitable and inclusive approaches to technological innovation and management. Woodrow has published works in influential practitioner-oriented publications such as INCOSE Insight Magazine, ACM Interactions, Fast Company Magazine, and The Conversation.

Introduction

Welcome to the first edition of The Diversity, Equity, and Inclusion Mindset in Project Management. We provide a roadmap to help project managers foster an equitable project team environment without barriers to opportunities, including developing an inclusive space where all team members feel welcomed, valued, respected, and engaged.

The Diversity, Equity, and Inclusion Mindset in Project Management primary goal are centered on exploring how to incorporate and advance diversity, equity, and inclusion principles, tools, and techniques throughout the five (5) major project management process groups:

- Initiating
- Planning
- Executing
- Monitoring and Controlling
- Closeout

We focus on developing the professional (nontechnical) skills, growth mindset, and systems perspective needed to lead projects effectively and equitably.

Upon successful completion of this book, you will be able to:
- Gain a foundational understanding of technical project management principles, tools, and techniques, including the five (5) major project management process groups.
- Gain fundamental knowledge of Diversity, Equity, and Inclusion (DE/I) principles, concepts, techniques, terms, and definitions.
- Develop a growth mindset by recognizing, identifying, and demonstrating the attitudes, beliefs, and behaviors that underpin the inclusive and equitable management of technical projects and cross-functional teams.
- Demonstrate the ability to engage a systems approach in applying a Diversity, Equity, and Inclusion (DE/I) mindset to managing technical projects and teams.
- Develop and apply the leadership and professional (nontechnical) skills required to be an inclusive and equitable technical project manager.

Book Approach

It's helpful to understand how it is organized and how to use the helpful tips throughout the book. Each chapter starts with the chapter overview and critical topics, outlining the key concepts you will learn for that chapter. We provide recommendations, checkpoints, and hints throughout each chapter to help you master the diversity, equity, and inclusion mindset.

- PMO Nerd Recommendations are advice and tips based on best practices and concepts.
- PMO Nerd Checkpoints provide context and explain exciting points in the material.
- PMO Nerd Hints are designed to drive critical thinking to apply material learned to your everyday life.

When you've finished reading the chapter, we provide a summary of key topics and concepts learned. It's helpful to apply the concepts you learn to real-world scenarios.

The Science and Art of Project Management

"Fundamentals of Project Management"

Chapter 1 Overview

This chapter focus on the fundamentals of project management principles, tools, and techniques, including the five major project management process groups: initiating, planning, executing, monitoring/controlling, and closeout. We walk you through the project management journey by focusing on the technical skills and knowledge required to lead projects and project teams.

Key Topics:

- Terms and Definition of Project Management
- Roles and Responsibilities of Project Managers
- Project Management Process Groups
- Project Management Knowledge Areas

The science and art of project management start with understanding the fundamentals of projects, project management, and the roles and responsibilities of project managers. We unlock the principles, tools, and techniques required to manage traditional (waterfall), hybrid, or agile projects. This chapter will focus on the technical approach to balance the project constraints (scope, cost, schedule, and quality) that can impact and influence your project results. You will learn the technical skills and knowledge required to lead projects and project teams.

Fundamentals of a Project

As we start your project management journey, let's define a project. A project is a product, service, or result produced for a customer, client, or project sponsor. There are two characteristics traits of a project; first, projects are temporary with a definite start and end date, and secondly, projects must produce a unique product, service, or result. There are many types of projects: aerospace, automotive, construction, consulting, energy, financial services, government, healthcare, utility, information technology, manufacturing, Etc. All private, public, commercial, and government industries develop and manage projects.

Obtaining project requirements and deliverables is essential to project success because they provide the project framework. Project requirements include but are not limited to scope, schedule, and cost. The goal is to define the project objectives, including budget and deadline. Project deliverables are approved outcomes that the project must satisfy to ensure the successful completion of the project. The goal is to produce the final "approved" product, service, or result for the customer, client, or project sponsor.

Project artifacts are documents that help manage, track, and report the project throughout the project cycle life. Understanding the requirements and deliverables required to plan, manage, and execute the project is essential to success.

> **PMO Nerd Hint:** Develop project goals around the project requirements and deliverables, i.e., scope, schedule, cost, and quality. Project goals will create an opportunity to collaborate and develop alignment between the project team and the customer, client, or project sponsor. What does success look like in achieving the project goal?

Roles and Responsibilities of Project Managers

The next step in your project management journey is understanding the roles and responsibilities of project managers. Project managers are the person charged and assigned by the performing organization to lead the project. Project managers primary responsibilities are planning and managing the project requirements and deliverables, including scope, schedule, cost, and quality. Project Managers are responsible for leading the project team, managing stakeholders, and guiding the project towards completion. Successful project managers must balance the science and art of project management to meet the project requirements and achieve the project deliverables.

> **PMO Nerd Checkpoint:** Project managers are accountable for project performance and the successful completion of the project, including meeting all deliverables and requirements for its customer, client, or project sponsor.

Terms and Definition of Project Management

The final step in your project management journey is understanding the definition of project management. Project management is the application of knowledge, skills, tools, and techniques to meet the project requirements and deliverables and help move a project towards completion.

> "Project management is defined as a collection of proven techniques for proposing, planning, implementing, managing, and evaluating projects, combined with the art of managing people."
>
> - American Society for Quality

Project management knowledge areas include but are not limited to scope, cost, and schedule, better known as the "Triple constraint." Triple constraint is a concept in project management that bases project success on cost (project budget), time (schedule for the project to reach completion), and scope (Task required to fulfill the project's goals). Let's take a deeper dive into scope, cost, and schedule.

Scope Management describes the work required to deliver a product, service, or result, including mapping out all the work needed to complete the project. Some aspects include the project scope statement, justification, objectives, restrictions, available resources, and stakeholders. Cost Management is a set of processes to ensure that the project is delivered within the approved budget, including the financial resources required. Cost management's primary goal is to provide a structured way to plan, estimate, determine and control costs.

Schedule Management is the set of processes required to ensure that the project is delivered on time, including meeting task/activity deadlines and the overall project schedule. Part of schedule management is the distribution of people, equipment, and materials among project activities. The triple constraint plays an essential part in any successful project, but there are additional project management knowledge areas critical to a project. We will discuss other project management knowledge areas later in chapter 1.

> **PMO Nerd Recommendation:** In addition to balancing cost, time, and scope, project managers must manage quality, risk, and benefit. You should take a holistic approach to project management by understanding the requirements and deliverables required to plan, manage, and execute the project.

The Science of Project Management

The science of project management is the processes, tools, and systemic approach to meet the project requirements. Another way to think about it is the science of project management is the technical approach to balance the project scope, schedule, cost, and quality. Project managers are to deliver the project on time, within budget, and according to the scope of work.

The first step to achieving this goal is identifying the acceptance criteria for project success. Acceptance criteria are performance requirements and deliverables agreed to and accepted by the customer, client, or project sponsor.

> **PMO Nerd Hint:** Schedule a meeting with the project team to review the project deliverables and acceptance criteria. Meeting with the project team is an opportunity to set priorities and develop a roadmap to achieve the project objectives and goals.

The Art of Project Management

The art of project management is the ability to apply your knowledge, nontechnical skills, and growth mindset to meet the project requirements. Another way to think about it, the art of project management focuses on the balance of people (project team), emotions, and conflict that can impact and influence the project indirectly. The first step to achieving this goal is identifying what success looks like outside the project scope, cost, and schedule. How do you interact with your customer, client, or project sponsor? How do you interact with your project team? Throughout your project management journey, we will provide you with principles, concepts, and techniques to help develop your nontechnical skills as a project manager, emphasizing creating an inclusive and diverse project team.

PMO Nerd Checkpoint: Collaborate with your project team and key stakeholders (customer, client, or project sponsor) and discuss everyone's communication style and conflict management approach.

The Science and Art of Project Management

The Science of Project Management	The Art of Project Management
Knowledge	People
Processes and Approach	Nontechnical Skills
Tools and Techniques	Emotions and Conflicts

Figure 1.0 _ The Science and Art of Project Management

In the second phase of your project management journey, you will learn more about project management methodologies and approaches, project management process groups, and project management knowledge areas.

Project Management Methodology and Approach

Many project management methodologies and approaches are helpful for project managers in planning and managing projects. The four most popular project management approaches are traditional/waterfall, agile, integrated project delivery, and program management.

As a project manager, it's essential to identify which project management approach fits project objectives and goals. We will focus on traditional, agile, and integrated project delivery.

Traditional Project Management Methodology

The traditional project approach is a sequential, linear process focusing on completing each project phase in sequential order. This approach consists of gathering detailed requirements, putting a plan together, and delivering the project requirements and deliverables. This method requires several phases and completing each phase before starting the next phase. Examples of phases are initiating, planning, executing, and closing. The traditional approach focuses on in-depth project planning, command, and control, including change control to manage changes.

> **PMO Nerd Checkpoint:** Some companies and organizations utilize project stage gates in their traditional project approach. Each project stage gate, i.e., Initiate Gate, Planning Gate, Execution Gate, and Close Gate, requires approval before advancing to the next gate.

Traditional Project Approach

INITIATING → PLANNING → EXECUTING → CLOSING

MONITORING & CONTROL

Figure 2.0 _ Traditional Project Approach

Agile Project Management Methodology

An agile project approach is an iterative approach focusing on continuous releases and incorporating customer feedback with every interaction. Each phase of the project is time-boxed and complete project features are delivered interactively. Agile project management focuses on high-level planning and control through inspections and adaptation. The two most popular agile approaches are Scrum and Kanban. Scrum is a framework that helps teams work together by encouraging groups to self-organize and commit to completing an increment of work.

Kanban is a framework that visualizes your work, limits work in progress, and maximizes efficiency. Agile approaches are lean, extreme, crystal, dynamic, and feature-driven development.

Agile Project Approach

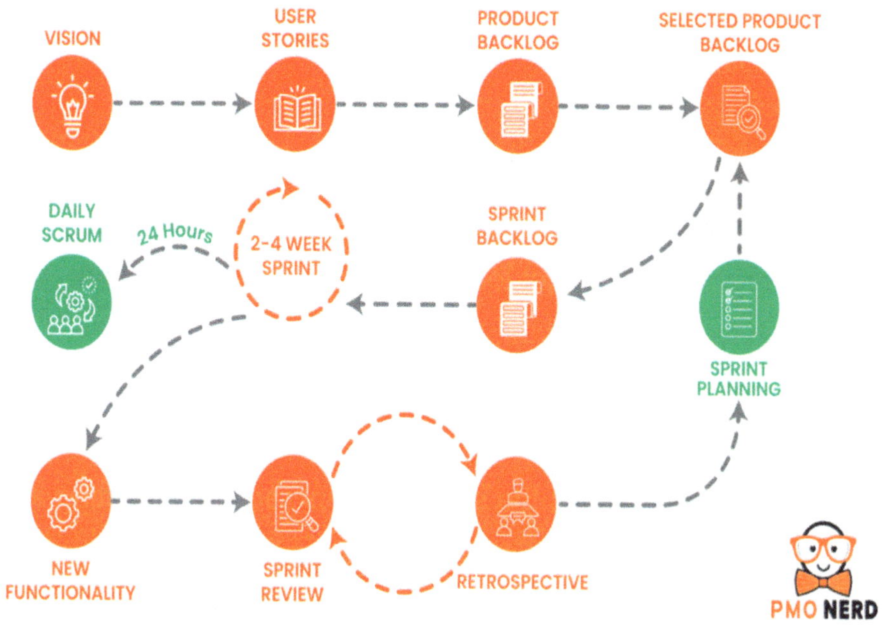

Figure 3.0 _ Agile Project Approach

Integrated Project Delivery Methodology

Integrated project delivery is a collaborative approach that seeks efficiency and involvement of all participants, i.e., people, business structures, and systems, throughout the project lifecycle.

The shared knowledge of all team members is essential to maximize the project outcomes. Collaboration benefits include continuous issue resolution, jointly developed targets, shared information systems, early involvement of stakeholders, and collaborative decision-making. This approach helps eliminate waste, empower the team, deliver faster results, build quality, and improve communication.

> **PMO Nerd Checkpoint:** To take advantage of the integrated project delivery approach, you must fully integrate the project teams, including all internal and external stockholders.

Programs and Portfolios

Program management is the strategic approach to executing and controlling multiple related projects. Like project management, program management is the application of knowledge, skills, tools, and techniques to meet the program requirements and deliverables. There are two characteristics traits of a program; first, programs consist of projects linked together through a shared deliverable. Secondly, programs must work towards achieving strategic business goals. Some benefits of program management are a comprehensive view of the organization's activities, helping achieve strategic goals, providing consistency, and sharing resources.

A portfolio is a collection of projects, programs, and operations managed as a group to achieve a strategic objective. Portfolio management is a centralized approach used by project managers and project management offices to manage and control one or more portfolios to ensure they align with the organization's overall strategic goals and objectives.

Project Management Office

A project management office is a management structure that standardizes the project-related governance processes and facilitates sharing of resources, methodologies, tools, and techniques. The project management office structure may change project managers' roles and responsibilities. Types of project management offices are supportive, controlling, and directive. The supportive project management office provides a consultative role to projects by supplying resources and processes. The controlling project management office provides support and requires compliance through various means. The directive project management office takes control of the projects by directly managing their projects.

There are multiple organizational structures within the project management office, i.e., functional, projectized, and matrix. Functional organization team members are group by specialty, and the project managers have little authority. Projectized organizations' team members are collocated, and the project manager has the power. Matrix organizations are a combination of functional and projectized, classified as weak matrix, balance matrix, and strong matrix. Identifying the resources available to help you plan and manage the project is essential.

Project Management Process Groups

Defining project management process groups are essential in your project management journey. Project management process groups are logical grouping of various project management knowledge, skills, tools, and techniques. This grouping of the process helps to achieve a specific project objective. The five project management process groups are initiating, planning, executing, monitoring/controlling, and closing.

Project Management Process Groups

Figure 4.0_ Project Management Process Groups

Initiating Process Group

The initiating phase sets the project's direction and authorizes the project manager to start. Some major activities are defining the initial business need, defining the initial scope of the project, and commitment of initial financial resources. The essential purpose of this process group is to align the customer, client, or project sponsor expectations with the project's requirements and deliverables.

Planning Process Group

The planning phases involve developing the strategy to achieve the project requirements and objectives, including establishing scope, cost, and schedule. Project managers set the course of action that enables easy stakeholder buy-in and engagement. The essential purpose of this process group is to develop a project management plan and the artifacts necessary to carry out the project activities.

Executing Process Group

In the executing phase, the project team gets to work producing the project's deliverables and objectives. Some significant activities include project teams carrying out their respective tasks, coordinating people resources, and managing stakeholders' expectations. The essential purpose of this process group is to complete the work defined in the project management plan, i.e., project requirements and deliverables.

Monitoring and Controlling Process Group

The monitoring and controlling phase track, review, and orchestrate all tasks and identify any areas in which change is required. Project managers ensure that the work is carried out according to the plan and meets the project requirements. The essential purpose of this process group is to measure project performance and analyze it at regular intervals.

Closing Process Group

The closing phase consists of processes performed to conclude all activities related to the entire project to ensure that the project is closed. Some significant activities include lessons learned, the release of project resources, and post-project review. The essential purpose of this process group is to obtain acceptance and close the project or phase.

> **PMO Nerd Checkpoint:** Project managers are responsible for satisfying the conditions for each phase and starting the next one. Before exiting a phase, they must be fully aware of the deliverables that must be completed and accepted by the concerned stakeholders.

Project Management Knowledge Areas

Project managers must balance the art and science of project management by mastering the project management knowledge areas throughout the project management process groups (i.e., project life cycle).

Integration Management

Integration management includes the process and activities to identify, define, combine, unify, and coordinate the various methods and project management activities.

Integration management has a project charter, project management plan, and integrated change control.

> **PMO Nerd Checkpoint:** Project managers are authorized to monitor and control the functions and activities taking place on the project. It's essential to verify or create a change control process to manage changes throughout the project lifecycle.

Scope Management

Scope management includes the processes required to ensure that the project consists of all the work required and only the work necessary to complete the project successfully. Scope management includes collecting requirements, defining scope, and validating scope. As the project transition from initiating to planning, it's essential to define the scope and validate the acceptance criteria.

Schedule Management

Schedule management includes the processes required to manage the project's timely completion. Schedule management includes defining activities, sequence activities, and estimating activity durations: critical understanding of deadlines and deliverable play's essential role in delivering the project on time.

Cost Management

Cost management includes the processes involved in planning, estimating, budgeting, financing, funding, managing, and controlling cost. It's essential to deliver the project within the approved budget.

Quality Management

Quality management is the degree to which the project and its components meet the customer, client, or project sponsor's expectations, objectives, and standards.

Resource Management

Resource management includes the processes that organize, manage, and lead the project team. Resource management includes planning resource management, estimating activity resources, and acquiring resources.

Communication Management

Communication management includes the processes required to ensure timely and appropriate planning, collection, creation, distribution, storage, retrieval, command, control, monitoring, and disposition of project information.

Risk Management

Risk management includes risk management planning, identification, analysis, response, and controlling risk on a project.

> **PMO Nerd Checkpoint:** Risk management is the probability of an unfavorable outcome or financial loss. The party that can best control the risk identified should be assigned to manage the risk.

Procurement Management

Procurement management includes the process necessary to purchase or acquire products, services, or results from outside the project team.

Stakeholder Management

Stakeholder management includes the process required to identify the people, groups, or organizations that could impact or be impacted by the project. As a project manager, engaging and managing stakeholders' expectations is essential to project management.

Project Manager Roles and Responsibilities throughout the Project Management Process Groups

In the final phase of your project management journey, you will learn project managers' roles and responsibilities based on best practices throughout the project management process groups. (it's essential to know the roles and responsibilities within your organization).

Initiating

The initiation phase is all about understanding the project. Project managers collaborate with key stakeholders, project sponsors, and the project team to obtain authorization to start. Key deliverables are the approved project budget and establishing the project scope. The project manager's role and responsibilities include but are not limited to:

- Review the Project Charter/Organizational Chart
- Review and Approve Project Funding
- Review Historical Project Data
- Conduct a Kickoff Meeting
- Identify Management Information System

PMO Nerd Hint: Project managers should document the project's goals, priorities, schedule, and budget, including uncovering project risks, constraints, and any factors that negatively impact the project.

Planning

The planning phase is an important and ongoing activity that happens throughout the life cycle of a project. Project managers are responsible for creating a project management plan to outline the actions required to be successful. The planning phase includes establishing the scope and refining the objectives to meet the project requirements, including developing a plan to manage the project risks, constraints, and priorities. The project manager's role and responsibilities include but are not limited to:

- Conduct Scope Review Meeting
- Identify Stakeholders
- Review Contract Agreements
- Developed a Project Management Plan (PMP)
- Create a Change Management Plan
- Create a Quality Management Plan

PMO Nerd Checkpoint: A project management plan is a working document that offers a blueprint to stakeholders surrounding the planning and execution of an upcoming project.

Executing

The executing phase objectives are to deliver the tasks, milestones, and deliverables required for the customer, client, or project sponsor.

Project managers manage teams effectively while orchestrating timeline expectations and spend most of their time on task management. The project manager's role and responsibilities include but are not limited to:
- The Science and Art of Project Management
- Execution of Scope, Cost, and Schedule
- Quality Management
- Stakeholder Engagement and Management
- Executing the Project Deliverables

Monitoring and Controlling

During the monitoring and controlling phase, the project manager is responsible for tracking, reviewing, and regulating progress. Project managers communicate the project progress with all stakeholders and provide an opportunity for the client to review the deliverables and provide feedback. The monitoring and controlling phase include identifying change areas and initiating the corresponding change as needed. The project manager's role and responsibilities include but are not limited to:
- Project Team Meetings & Reports
- Stakeholder Team Meetings & Reports
- Tracking Cost and Schedule Performance
- Integrated Change Control
- Managing Risk

Closing

Finally, the closing phase is the last step. After clients are satisfied with the results and sign-off on the deliverables, it is time to close the project officially. Project managers are responsible for the handover of deliverables, vendors/resources released, analyzing performance, and so forth. The most critical responsibility is formally closing the project and analyzing project team performance. The project manager's role and responsibilities include but are not limited to:

- Conduct a Walk-thru/Acceptance Meeting
- Create a Close Out Checklist
- Conduct a Closeout Meeting
- Closing Out the Project
- Lesson Learned

Chapter 1 Summary

This chapter focused on the fundamentals of project management principles, tools, and techniques, including project management methodology and approaches. Project management is the process by which a project is planned, tracked, controlled, reported, and executed. We unlock the roles and responsibilities of project managers throughout the five major project management process groups. Project managers are accountable and responsible for planning and managing a project along with the project team to produce the desired deliverables for a customer, client, or project sponsor.

Key Topics:
- Terms and Definition of Project Management
- Roles and Responsibilities of Project Managers
- Project Management Process Groups
- Project Management Knowledge Areas

Fundamentals of Diversity, Equity, and Inclusion

"The Inclusive Mindset"

Chapter 2 Overview

This chapter focus on the fundamentals of Diversity, Equity, and Inclusion principles, tools, and techniques, including an understanding of empathy and microaggression in the Workplace. We emphasize creating an inclusive project environment and diverse project teams.

Key Topics:
- Terms and Definition of Diversity, Equity, Inclusion, and Justice
- Equality vs. Equity
- Creating an Inclusive Project Environment
- Empathy and Microaggressions in the Workplace
- Racial Privilege and Racial Oppression

Our experiences shape our views on diversity, equity, and inclusion in life, including socially, economically, and spiritly. Developing a "Diversity, Equity, and Inclusion Mindset" starts with understanding the principles, concepts, and definitions of diversity, equity, and inclusion. This chapter will focus on creating an inclusive project environment and a diverse project team by incorporating diversity, equity, and inclusion techniques in project management.

Diversity, Equity, and Inclusion

Diversity, Equity, and Inclusion can be a challenging field to navigate as it continues to evolve. Project managers are focused on delivering the project on time and within budget; however, creating an inclusive project environment is essential. Understanding diversity, equity, and inclusion definitions are the first step to navigating your journey.

The first step in creating an inclusive project environment is diversity. Diversity encompasses the range of similarities and differences everyone brings to the workplace. Types of diversity include but are not limited to National Origin, Language, Race and Color, Disability, Ethnicity, Gender, Age, Religion and Belief, Sexual Orientation, Gender Identity, Socioeconomic Status, Veteran Status, and Family structure.

PMO Nerd Checkpoint: Diversity acknowledges, celebrates, and catalyzes different characteristics, values, beliefs, experiences, backgrounds, and behaviors.

"By fostering a culture of diversity —or a capacity to appreciate and value individual differences —employers' benefit from varied perspectives on how to confront business challenges and achieve success."

- U.S. Department of labor

The second step in creating an inclusive project environment is equity. Equity prioritizes all individuals' fair and impartial treatment, access, opportunity, and advancement. Equity is about recognizing that everyone is unique, and it's important to accommodate their needs adequately.

PMO Nerd Recommendation: As a project manager, it's your duty and responsibility to understand your project team's strengths and weaknesses. Create a roadmap to support each team member and accommodate their needs adequately. Your focus must be on the fair and impartial treatment of all project team members.

The third step in creating an inclusive project environment is inclusion. Inclusion is an organizational effort and practice in which different groups or individuals having different backgrounds are culturally and socially accepted and welcomed. Inclusion creates and sustains an environment that supports direction, alignment, and commitment from everyone in your organization.

> **PMO Nerd Checkpoint:** Inclusion cultures make people feel respected and valued for who they are as individuals or groups. All team members should be engaged and participate regardless of position and title.

The last step in creating an inclusive project environment is justice. Justice is a systemic approach to fixing the issue at the root cause. Another way to think about justice is the action behind the words and when companies and organizations focus on Diversity, Equity, and Inclusion.

> **PMO Nerd Checkpoint:** Equity and Justice are required for real change and impact. Equity is a solution for addressing imbalanced social systems. Justice can take equity one step further by fixing the systems to lead to long-term, sustainable, equitable access for generations to come.

When diversity, equity, and inclusion are prioritized on your project, every facet can benefit, including problem-solving, improving products and services, and understanding the customer better. Diversity, equity, and inclusion provide a broader perspective for problem-solving and developing creative solutions for a competitive advantage and greater success. Diversity, equity, and inclusion create and foster an open, learning environment for the betterment of your employees, which ultimately produces quality products and services for your customers. More likely to understand target customers when they have at least one member who represents their target's gender, race, age, sexual orientation, or culture

> **PMO Nerd Recommendation:** Customers, clients, and project sponsors come from diverse backgrounds; therefore, a diverse project team could help provide a unique view on meeting the project requirements and deliverables.

Inclusive Project Environment

An inclusive project environment is cooperative, collaborative, open, fair, and accountable. The project team feels valued, respected, and engaged. More importantly, each team member can effectively participate and bring unique talents, skills, and perspectives.

To create an inclusive project environment, everyone needs to have a place and be able to speak out from there. These are not always comfortable conversations, but they are vital for the growth of the project team. The most critical part of creating an inclusive project environment is practicing it daily. These micro-moments add up to create a culture of fairness and belonging. There are endless benefits to creating an inclusive project environment. Diversity, Equity, and Inclusion are actions that establish awareness and transform mindsets, behaviors, and practices to develop and sustain a diverse, equitable, and inclusive environment.

Diversity, Equity, and Inclusion Framework
A framework will help address the issue at its core, help people process your "why" findings, and then offer an action plan for how the company can provide equal growth opportunities for everyone. Knowledge and action can help with healing. Frameworks are essential because they create a structure and guide building diversity, equality, and inclusion in the workplace. The diversity, equity, and inclusion framework focus on four key areas, understanding, healing, learning, and discussion.

Equity vs. Equality

Equality and equity are essential in the project and the project team. Equality gives all individuals fair treatment and the same resources or opportunities. On the other hand, equity recognizes that each person has different circumstances and allocates the exact resources and opportunities needed to reach an equal outcome.

Interaction Institute for Social Change

Figure 5.0 _ Interaction Institute for Social Change
Source: "Interaction Institute for Social Change Artist: Angus Maguire."

PMO Nerd Checkpoint: Equality refers to the same blanket of privileges, rules, and opportunities applied to all employees, and these aggregates already present inequality rather than eliminating unconscious bias and other bases.

Empathy and Microaggressions

Empathy is the ability to identify, relate and share similar feelings or emotions another person may be experiencing. Three types of empathy are cognitive empathy, somatic empathy, and affective empathy. Cognitive empathy involves understanding people's mentality and how a situation may influence their thoughts. It relates to the theory of mind, which is the ability of someone to think like others and predict future behaviors. Somatic empathy produces a physical response to what someone is feeling or experiencing.

Affective empathy involves knowing and understanding how to respond to a person's emotions. Compassion in the workplace is crucial because it creates an environment of openness and transparency, and people are encouraged to share their opinions and feel they will be treated fairly.

Microaggressions are the everyday slights, insults, putdowns, invalidations, and offensive behaviors that people experience in daily interactions with generally well-intentioned individuals who may be unaware that they have engaged in demeaning ways. Three microaggressions in the workplace are Color Blindness, Lack of Acknowledgment, and Mansplaining.

- Color Blindness Microaggressions: Denies people of different colors their race-related experience.
- Acknowledgment Microaggressions: Not acknowledging someone's intelligence or not creating their work.
- Mansplaining Microaggressions: It happens when a male coworker forcibly tries to convey something to a female. Even if the female didn't ask about it, she might have more knowledge than he does. This concept applies to race as well.

Tokenism and Race

Tokenism is common in businesses that only view diversity to improve their public image. Work isn't valued on its merit. Tokenism can lead to imposter syndrome, stress, and further discrimination. Tokenism doesn't respect the job or the person—only what they represent while present and doing it. Hiring employees from underrepresented groups means nothing if they're not in positions of power and don't have a voice.

Five Ways to Avoid Tokenism:
1. Incorporate diversity as a policy
2. Measure impact over the percentage
3. Avoid tokenizing your photographs
4. Diverse options and accommodations
5. Hire and empower diverse candidates

Racial Justice

Race is a socially constructed system of categorizing humans primarily based on observable physical features (phenotypes), such as skin color and ancestry. Racial justice is the systematic fair treatment of people of all races, resulting in equitable opportunities and outcomes for everyone.

> **PMO Nerd Recommendation:** Project managers can promote racial justice with transparency about policies and progress. You do not need all the answers but must bring compassion to conversations. Listen first and lead with empathy.

Racial Privilege and Racial Oppression

Racial privilege describes race-based advantages and preferential treatment based on skin color. Racial oppression refers to race-based disadvantages, discrimination, and exploitation based on skin color. Race, gender, social-economic class, and other classifications have privileges and face oppression.

> **PMO Nerd Hint:** Project managers should recognize the privileges and oppression within the project team. Have open conversations and develop strategies to remove barriers and create an equitable environment.

Chapter 2 Summary

This chapter focused on the fundamentals of Diversity, Equity, and Inclusion principles, tools, and techniques. Understanding how empathy, microaggressions, tokenism, and race plays in project management is essential. Diversity and inclusion efforts are a necessary & vital piece of a successful project culture that fosters equality amongst all project team members.

Key Topics:
- Terms and Definition of Diversity, Equity, Inclusion, and Justice
- Equality vs. Equity
- Creating an Inclusive Project Environment
- Empathy and Microaggressions in the Workplace
- Racial Privilege and Racial Oppression

Social Identity Influence in Project Management

Chapter 3 Overview

This chapter focus on the growth mindset as a project manager by recognizing, identifying, and demonstrating the attitudes, beliefs, and behaviors that underpin the inclusive and equitable management of technical projects and cross-functional teams.

Key Topics:

- Terms and Definition of Social Identities
- Benefits of Self-Reflection
- Self-Reflection Activity
- Social Identity Influence on the Project Team
- Pros and Cons of Culture Fit
- Social Identity Influence on Managing and Performance

Creating an inclusive project environment starts with you! Project managers lead diverse and inclusive project teams, including planning and managing the project requirements and deliverables for customers, clients, and project sponsors. It's important to recognize and identify your attitudes, beliefs, and behaviors that can impact and influence the project team's performance. This chapter will focus on self-reflection techniques to underpin the inclusive and equitable management skills required to create an inclusive project environment.

Terms and Definition of Social Identities

Social identity is the framework to help project managers recognize and identify the attitudes, beliefs, and behaviors that can impact and influence the project team's performance. Social identities are the labels people use to categorize or identify themselves and others as members of specific groups. Social identity groups are usually defined by some individuals' physical, social, and mental characteristics. Social identities include race/ethnicity, gender, social class/socioeconomic status, sexual orientation, disabilities, and religion/religious beliefs. Everyone has multiple social identities, and different combinations impact individuals' lived experiences. Each of us as individuals perceives the world through our social identity. We describe identity as "The way a person perceives, the way the world perceives them, and the qualities that characterize them."

PMO Nerd Checkpoint: Social identities are powerful because, as people, we categorize ourselves and each other into groups along social identity lines.

More specifically, social identities are a particular sort of identity that "come from shared conceptions and social relations" based on societal standards created by humans. Society determines which identities are flagged and which differences matter. Specific social identities feel more prominent in certain situations and contexts. Our social identities do not disappear when we go to work. Instead, they guide our collaboration and frequently decide who has access to authority within the organization.

Social Identities are dynamic, multiple, sociological, and silent. Social identities may be chosen or born into, visible or invisible, stable, or shifting. Think about how you identify as you read the following list:

- Race: A social construct that describes groups of people with physical characteristics (such as skin color, bone structure, hair texture, etc.).
- Gender: A social and legal position, as well as a set of societal expectations for actions, traits, and viewpoints based on one's perceived sexual organs.
- Age: The way that society categorizes people into various age groups.

- Development: The wide range of variations in one's physical, mental, cognitive, developmental, learning, and/or emotional make-up is known as one's ability. It also covers mental health and the effects of traumatic and abusive social situations.
- Sexual Orientation: A person's attraction to other people on a physical and sexual level, or their lack thereof.
- Religion: Beliefs in a god or gods, as well as identification with a specific religion or set of spiritual practices held by an individual or group of individuals.
- Class: A person's or a group's social standing as indicated by their level of education, income, and vocation.

People are classified in an infinite number of ways over time. Examining the social identities that have the most significant impact on people's lives is beneficial.
Self-reflection can help create an inclusive project environment by removing barriers and creating allyships. Understanding and identifying your culture/identity is the first step of self-reflection.

Benefits of Self-Reflection
Self-reflection helps project managers and leaders recognize and identify the values, feelings, and potential blind spots that can create barriers between you and your project team.

These barriers can lead to stereotypes, bias, prejudice, and discrimination if left unchecked.

> **PMO Nerd Checkpoint:** Stereotypes are preconceived ideas that generalize members of a group. Bias is a personal preference, like or dislike, that can interfere with your ability to be objective. Prejudice is what an individual thinks, and discrimination is an action based on prejudice.

Project Manager and Project Team

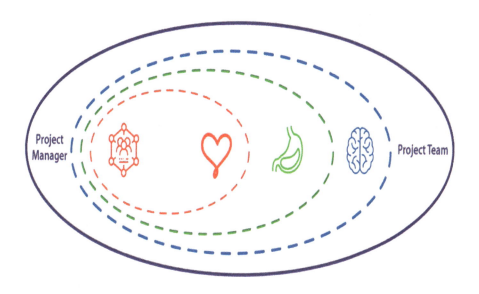

Figure 6.0_Project Manager and Project Team

Self-Reflection Activity

This activity helps project managers and leaders develop identity self-awareness and social-emotional awareness before/during entering a context to practice empathy. The goal is to move from "transactional empathy" to "transformational empathy."

Self-Reflection: **Values**

What values do you feel strongly about or live by (e.g., family, creativity, social justice, friends, love, and money)? These are what drive your actions. Please list your top three values.

Self-Reflection: **Feelings**

How are you feeling reflecting on identity, emotions, and values? Try to identify where these feelings are coming from. How might these feelings affect your empathy work? Please list your top three feelings.

Self-Reflection: **Potential Blind spots**

What parts of your identities, values, emotions, or lived experience might obstruct your ability to fully empathize and authenticate with your context and the people within it? Please list your top three blind spots.

> **PMO Nerd Checkpoint:** Cultural competency is the human behavior that incorporates communication, action, beliefs, thoughts, and values of ethnicity, ethnic background, religious beliefs, and social values.

Social Identity Influence on Hiring

Social identities can play a role in hiring because, as people, we categorize ourselves and each other into groups along social identity lines. If you are unaware, you can create stereotypes, bias, prejudice, and discrimination towards a group.

> **PMO Nerd Checkpoint:** Implicit bias is attitudes or stereotypes that unconsciously affect our understanding, actions, and decisions.

Successful firms consider and prioritize diversity, equity, and inclusion to promote a thriving workplace and meet the requirements of everyone engaged. When incorporating diversity, equity, and inclusion, your hiring procedures are the most excellent place to start. Techniques to improve hiring practices:

- Strategic Outreach and Recruitment: Outreach and recruitment start with technical leaders attending and recruiting from all segments of society.

- Diversity and Inclusion Hiring Committee: Develop a diversity and inclusion hiring committee that focuses on a data-driven approach. Develop diverse interview panel guidance and require hiring managers to certify that it was followed for all selections.
- Manager Flow Data: Collect, analyze, and measure the hiring manager data. Identify key performance indicators that measure success. Develop a Scorecard to display the data on who is hired and promoted.
- Weighted Evaluation: Develop a weighted evaluation that focuses on the core responsibilities of candidates. Recognize the "unconscious bias" in behavior interview questions.

PMO Nerd Recommendation: Outreach and recruitment are not limited to new candidates; develop a strategy to recruit and promote within your organization. What is the career path for someone who wants to transition into project management?

PMO Nerd Hint: Hiring plays an essential role in project management because you are responsible for "forming" your project team. You want a diverse and inclusive project team that can deliver the project on time and within budget.

Recruiting tactics are used by businesses and organizations to find, attract, and hire individuals in their hiring cultures. Depending on the values they look for in potential employees, each organization tackles the hiring process differently, and a company's hiring culture frequently mirrors the company's culture.

Project Culture

The people and leadership shape project culture. On the one hand, project managers can create a positive and inclusive culture. On the other hand, project managers can create a harmful and toxic culture.

> "Culture fit is the likelihood that someone will reflect and/or be able to adopt to the core beliefs, attitudes, and behaviors that make up your organization."
> - Harvard Business Review

Culture Fit Pros and Cons

Pros	Cons
Dedicated Workers	Low Retention
Saves money	Draw Attention to Personality
Business Promotion	False Pretense

Figure 7.0_ Culture Fit Pros and Cons

A positive work environment attracts quality candidates. Many job searchers appreciate business culture more than money because most people wouldn't apply for a job at a company that didn't share their values. When unhappy at work, employees are less likely to be satisfied with their jobs and more inclined to search for alternative employment. Putting your culture on display and assessing candidates for culture fit are both parts of the hiring process. However, another aspect to this is less blatant but just as significant. Building a culture that will draw the best talent out there is involved. Cultural differences influence people's interactions with their workplace's internal and exterior environments.

Offering these perks while attracting qualified applicants to your company and using a well-thought-out recruiting strategy can result in quality recruits, increased productivity, and ultimately higher customer happiness. It is essential to employee engagement, performance, and productivity; cultural fit is very significant. Employees that feel more a part of their work are happier, have higher levels of job satisfaction, are more devoted, work more, and are more likely to stick with their organization. Cultural compatibility is crucial for this reason. There are several benefits and drawbacks to cultural fit that affect employment.

> **PMO Nerd Recommendation:** Developing a diverse and inclusive culture starts with evaluating and assessing your current culture. Collect, analyze, and measure data, including creating a scorecard to display and communicate the data. Data is an essential step in evaluating your current culture.

Social Identity Influence on the Project Team

The more closely people connect with a group, the more it influences how individuals feel about themselves. Gaining status inside the group can help people feel more confident, fulfilled, and respected since being a member of that group becomes significant for how a person views themselves and their talents. Social identity is substantial because it affects how individuals perceive and behave around others. People are more likely to relate well to others in that group and feel good about themselves if they have a favorable perspective of their identity. Workplaces significantly impact employees' psychological states, which in turn affects their productivity, job satisfaction, and general well-being. Further investigation into how the employee's identity appears in social settings would be relevant and valuable. The entire cognitive system of the self-comprises the social self, distinct from the personalized self, and both combined.

In other words, if a person socially identifies with their employment, the social element of the workplace can add a crucial degree to the individual's self-esteem. Social identities can create "code-switching" to fit into the social group. Think code-switching beyond the use of language. You are not bringing your holistic self and changing your personality to "fit in." Change your body language to make others feel comfortable.

> **PMO Nerd Checkpoint:** Social identities have the most significant impact when people place a high value on belonging to a particular group and have deep emotional connections to that group. Self-esteem is conferred through group membership and thus aids in maintaining social identity.

Some of these tactics might be helpful to you even though not all of them are acceptable for every group or organization. You can also come up with your tactics to suit your circumstances.
Take note of the organization's depiction of social identities. Observe how social identities are expressed in your workplace and organization.

Is there diversity in your organization, but the people who make the decisions are less diverse? Is there diversity among people who make decisions but less among those with power?

Do specific social identities have variety while others do not? Once you've identified who is absent, think about how you can better reflect the social identities you don't hear from. Promote frequent communication among social identities. Promoting interaction amongst those belonging to various social identification groups is one of the most straightforward and well-proven methods for reducing prejudice and stereotyping. Think about the social identity groups that don't frequently interact in your current workplace and how you may create opportunities for them (e.g., projects, social events, retreats, or team-building activities). Raise equity by utilizing your comprehension of social identities. Giving people the resources, they need to achieve is what equity is all about (in comparison to equality, which is about giving everyone the same resources). When considering diversity and inclusion in businesses, equity is a crucial issue to keep in mind; without equality, initiatives may be less successful or even come off as tone-deaf.

Imposter Syndrome for Historical Marginal Groups
As previously established, the workplace is fundamentally a social setting. Any amplify discriminatory message historical marginal groups receive in the workplace can lead to imposter syndrome. Imposter syndrome is the lack of self-confidence, anxiety, and doubts about your thoughts, abilities, achievements, and accomplishments.

PMO Nerd Checkpoint: Imposter syndrome can lead to negative self-talk, feelings of inadequacy, dwelling on past mistakes, and not feeling good enough.

Project Team Personality

Project team members can change their behavior at work, play to their strengths, work on their flaws, interact with co-workers more successfully, and ultimately succeed in their job by better understanding their personalities. The personality mix impacts the efficacy of a team. A team that lacks relationship-builders won't function well together. When too many people of that personality type are on a team, harmony may be given an undue amount of importance, preventing anyone from pointing out weak ideas or unachievable deadlines. Numerous analyses on the ideal combination of personalities for a productive team exist.

Three personality attributes are shared among influential team members: the courage to push others, the capacity to ask uncomfortable questions, and the readiness to accept criticism. Team effectiveness is enhanced if these personality traits are present in every group member.

Five Personality Traits

Examining the so-called "big five" personality qualities is another technique to assess how personalities affect teams.

- Openness to experience: Individuals who rate highly on this trait are receptive to novel concepts and methods.
- Agreeability: Agreeableness is a personality trait described as cooperative, polite, kind, and friendly. People like to hang out with people who are more pleasant than themselves, and high scorers are selected, empathetic, and loving.
- Neuroticism: A high score here is not good. It denotes a person who struggles with emotion control, is prone to worry and depression, and is likely low on self-worth.
- Conscientiousness: Conscientiousness is a fundamental personality trait that reflects the tendency to be responsible, organized, hard-working, goal-directed, and to adhere to norms and rules. High achievers in this trait are dependable, organized, self-controlled, and reliable.
- Extroversion: A personality trait or style characterized by a preference for or orientation to engaging socially with others. Extroverts enjoy engaging with others and are outgoing, forceful, and confident in their social skills. Even though they enjoy being around others, introverts are more introspective and find it draining.

Social Identity Influence on Managing and Performance

Social Identity Influence on Managing and Performance Project managers are responsible and accountable for creating an inclusive project environment where all employees feel welcomed, valued, and respected. Social identity can influence "who" we promote; and incorrectly justify the "why." What does success look like? Does your definition of success influence your attitudes, beliefs, and behaviors? As leaders, we must recognize how unconscious bias can create barriers and play an essential role in engaging and managing our team.

> **PMO Nerd Checkpoint:** Unconscious Bias and underlying attitudes and stereotypes that people unconsciously attribute to another person or group of people affect how they understand and engage with a person or group.

Favoritism

Favoritism is when someone in a leadership position demonstrates favor toward one employee over others. Favoritism is usually unrelated to their job performance and instead occurs due to a personal bond or friendship shared between the two. Social identity can influence whom you favorite and incorrectly justify the "why." Some relationships develop faster than others, but your responsibility as a project manager is to be fair and equal when leading the project team.

> **PMO Nerd Recommendation:** Identify key performance indicators that measure success. Create a dashboard and provide actionable management data in an easy-to-read format. More importantly, building relationships will become each member and create a path to success.

Interpretation

Social identity can positively or negatively impact and influences your interpretation of someone's behaviors and actions. Depending on someone's social identity, you may misinterpret their body language or actions. As you build relationships with your project team, focus on getting to know their personalities, how they react to conflict, and handle stress. Don't rush to judgment, and always take a positive approach.

Chapter 3 Summary

This chapter focus on the growth mindset as a project manager by recognizing, identifying, and demonstrating the attitudes, beliefs, and behaviors that underpin the inclusive and equitable management of technical projects and cross-functional teams. We unlock the importance of understanding how stereotypes, bias, prejudice, and discrimination can impact the project team. Social identities play a role in hiring, managing, and leading a project team, including the "big five" personality qualities.

Key Topics:
- Terms and Definition of Social Identities
- Benefits of Self-Reflection
- Self-Reflection Activity
- Social Identity Influence on the Project Team
- Pros and Cons of Culture Fit
- Social Identity Influence on Managing and Performance

Creating a Winning Team

"Diversity in Project Management"

Chapter 4 Overview

This chapter focuses on a system approach to incorporate diversity, equity, and inclusion principles, tools, and techniques throughout the initiating and planning groups. We emphasize creating ground rules through collaboration and team development to help develop a commitment to creating an inclusive project environment.

Key Topics:

- Vision, Mission Statement, Values, and Goals
- SWOT Analysis and Assessment
- Diversity, Equity, and Inclusion Strategic Plan
- Work Breakdown Structure (WBS)

The first step of creating an inclusive project environment starts with incorporating diversity, equity, and inclusion at project management's initiating and planning stages. This chapter will focus on creating ground rules, collaboration, and team strategy planning around diversity, equity, and inclusion at the project level.

Project Management Process Groups (Initiating)

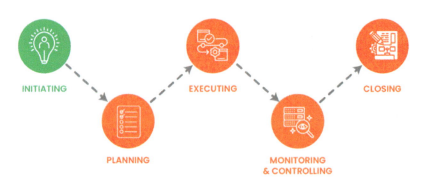

Figure 8.0_Project Management Process Groups

Initiating Process Group

The purpose of the initiating process is to start the project formally. It is necessary to remember that the commencement of the process cannot begin until after getting approval from the customer, client, or project sponsor.

During this process, the preliminary scope is defined, the financial capital (budget) is approved and released, and resources are available.

> **PMO Nerd Checkpoint:** If the project comprises several phases, each phase is required approval before formally starting.

The project manager's role and responsibilities for initiating are:
- Review the Project Charter
- Review and approve Project Funding
- Create a Project Organizational Chart
- Review Historical Project Data
- Conduct a Kickoff Meeting
- Identify Management Information System

Diversity, Equity, and Inclusion Vision, Mission Statement, Values, and Goals

Developing a diversity, equity, and inclusion vision is the first step in creating an inclusive project environment. Vision statements describe the long-term diversity and inclusion goals for the project team. Project managers should involve all project team members at every level of the organization to encourage alignment and adoption.

Critical elements of a good vision statement are:
- Forward-looking
- Motivating and inspirational
- Reflective of a project's team culture and core values
- Aimed at bringing benefits and improvements to the organization in the future

Refrain from using buzzwords, jargon, or vague statements. An example of diversity, equity, and inclusion vision statement is:

> "Our project team is talented, diverse, and committed to fostering a safe, fair, and inclusive workplace."

Creating a diversity, equity, and inclusion mission statement is essential in creating an inclusive project environment. Mission statements excite what the project team does and motivate them to become part of the organization. Critical elements of a good mission statement are:
- Motivating Employees
- Inspiring Customers
- Strategic Planning
- Setting Values

An example of diversity, equity, and inclusion mission statement is:

> "To foster a culture that exemplifies teamwork, embraces innovation, and values diversity, equity, and inclusion to achieve project excellence."

Creating and collaborating on diversity, equity, and inclusion values and goals is essential in creating an inclusive project environment. Project team values include group collaboration, group loyalty, and group Initiative. Creating a winning team is built on trust and respect for each other; therefore, your goals must be centered on inclusion. An example of diversity, equity, and inclusion goal is:

> "Our project team goals are to create an inclusive and supported work environment by respecting everyone's opinions and views."

Diversity, Equity, and Inclusion SWOT Analysis

The next step in creating an inclusive project environment is developing diversity, equity, and inclusion SWOT Analysis. SWOT stands for "strengths, weakness, opportunities, and threats." Strengths are things that your organization does particularly well or in a way that distinguishes you from your competitors.

Weaknesses, like strengths, are inherent features of your organization, so focus on your people, resources, systems, and procedures. Opportunities are openings or chances for something positive to happen, but you'll need to claim them yourself! Threats include anything that can negatively affect your business from the outside, such as supply-chain problems, shifts in market requirements, or a shortage of recruits.

> **PMO Nerd Checkpoint:** A SWOT analysis is a simple and practical framework for identifying strengths, weaknesses, opportunities, and threats that a company faces. It is essential to leverage strengths, minimize threats, and take advantage of available opportunities.

A SWOT analysis can help project managers understand how the project is positioned as it is related to diversity, equity, and inclusion. Creating a diversity, equity, and inclusion SWOT Analysis starts with gathering the project team, including people from various functions and levels in your organization. The project team will use brainstorming techniques to build a list of ideas about where your organization currently stands. A diversity, equity, and inclusion SWOT Assessment Questionnaire is a great opportunity to measure your project team's strengths and weaknesses. Example Diversity, Equity, and Inclusion SWOT Assessment Questionnaire.

SWOT Assessment Questions: Strengths
- What diversity, equity, and inclusion advantages does your project team have?
- What unique diversity, equity, and inclusion approach do your project team?
- What positive consumer perception does your project team have?

SWOT Assessment Questions: Weaknesses
- What does your project team not do well regarding diversity, equity, and inclusion?
- What weaknesses do your project team see in consumers, clients, or project sponsors?
- What factors contribute to diversity, equity, and inclusion image?

SWOT Assessment Questions: Opportunities
- What good opportunities are available in the diversity, equity, and inclusion marketplace?
- What are some diversity, equity, and inclusion resources that your company can capitalize on?
- Are there any changes in technology or markets that your company can take advantage of?

SWOT Assessment Questions: Threats
- What diversity, equity, and inclusion obstacles does your company face?
- What are your competitors doing better than you?
- Do changes in lifestyle, social patterns, Etc., pose a threat to your project team?

Team Charter, Roles and Responsibilities, and Effectiveness

Developing a team charter is an essential step in collaboration. A team charter is a document that outlines why the team has been brought together for the project. Project managers' responsibilities are to define teams' goals, establish clear guidelines, and set clear expectations. A RACI Matrix is a significant artifact in developing the team roles and responsibilities.

> **PMO Nerd Checkpoint:** The RACI Matrix is a system that brings structure and clarity to assigning the roles people play within a team. It is a simple grid system that you can use to clarify people's responsibilities and ensure that everything the team needs to do.

Team effectiveness plays an essential role in creating an inclusive project environment. Team effectiveness is the capacity of a team must accomplish the goals or objectives administered by an authorized organization. Effectiveness is a quality that leads the team to enhance performance, increase willingness to work together and improve the overall outcome. Components of team effectiveness are:

- Psychological Safety
- Trust
- Clarity
- Meaning
- Impact

Techniques to improve team effectiveness are establishing ground rules and communication. Ground rules establish clear expectations regarding acceptable behavior by project team members, including code of conduct, communication, working together, and meeting etiquette. Establish verbal and nonverbal communications, i.e., team meetings, one-on-one interactions, and water cooler conversations.

> **PMO Nerd Recommendation:** Project managers must communicate what success looks like outside of scope, cost, and schedule. What are the team expectations to interact with each other? Have an open conversation about nonverbal communication.

Project Management Process Groups (Planning)

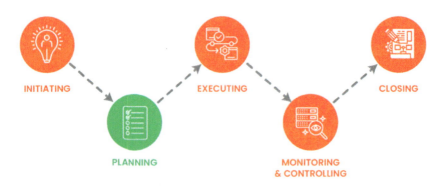

Figure 9.0_Project Management Process Groups

Planning Process Group

The purpose of the planning phase is to detail what was defined in the initiating step. Project managers are responsible for developing the project, including creating a project management plan. This phase requires the scope of work to be defined and detailed.

It is necessary to establish the value of the investment and the term of the project, how the work will be organized, the communication strategy, and the team members who will execute it. A framework for reviewing and controlling the plan is also set up. The project manager's role and responsibilities for planning are:

- Conduct Scope Review Meeting
- Identify Stakeholders
- Review Contract Agreements
- Developed a Project Management Plan (PMP)
- Create a Change Management Plan
- Create a Quality Management Plan

During the initiating phase, the project team developed a diversity, equity, and inclusion vision, mission statement, and goals, including diversity, equity, and inclusion SWOT assessment. Let's discuss the strategies to incorporate diversity, equity, and inclusion in the planning phase.

Diversity, Equity, and Inclusive Strategic Plan
A diversity, equity, and inclusion strategic plan are a roadmap designed to reach the project goal successfully, including defining its strategy and direction and making decisions on allocating its resources to pursue inclusive project environment objectives.

Six Key Elements of Strategic Planning are:
1. SWOT Assessment
2. Organization Environment Profile
3. Vision, Mission, and Values
4. Winning Strategy Development
5. Strategic Objectives
6. Strategic Check-ins

Strategy Formulation is the process of formulating a strategy, and a company will first assess its current situation by performing an internal and external audit. Strategy Implementation is Effective strategy implementation involves developing a solid structure, or framework, for implementing the strategy, maximizing the utilization of relevant resources, and redirecting marketing efforts in line with the strategy's goals and objectives. Strategy Evaluation is Reviewing the internal and external factors affecting the implementation of the system, measuring performance, and taking corrective steps to make the strategy more effective.

> **PMO Nerd Checkpoint:** Strategic Planning helps formulate better strategies using a logical, systematic approach. Enhanced communication between project team members and empowers individuals working in the organization.

A robust diversity, equity, and inclusion strategy should foster a culture of inclusion and engagement by employing culture change strategies. Emphasize the importance of inclusive diversity efforts by utilizing various communication strategies and tools demonstrating their support for these initiatives. Foster a diverse, high-performing workforce using data-driven approaches to promotion opportunities and career development. Find Out How Employees Feel! This may seem like an obvious step in launching a diversity, equity, and inclusion strategic planning, but it's often overlooked. By encouraging people to express their vision and inspiring them to act, leaders support and help followers achieve their goals. You wants to ensure that the roadmap and activities planned are meeting your team's needs and expectations. It's also important to set milestone check-ins with your employees to gauge the effectiveness of your diversity and inclusion exercises and overall employee satisfaction levels with the larger diversity, equity, and inclusion initiative.

PMO Nerd Recommendation: Print and circulate a DEI survey in the office and set up a dropbox where employees can deliver their surveys anonymously. Create employee engagement groups to encourage sharing their experiences and providing candid feedback.

Goals of Diversity, Equity, and Inclusive Strategic Plan

A diversity, equity, and inclusion strategy must define the project team's purpose, mission, and values. A plan must list the relevant metrics and establish a governance body that will own the diversity, equity, and inclusion initiatives.

A diversity, equity, and inclusion strategic plan aim to develop and incorporate organizational structures and business processes to promote teamwork, collaboration, cross-functional operations, and transparency. One of the most critical steps in developing a strategic plan is aligning diversity, equity, and inclusion processes and procedures with KPIs.

> **PMO Nerd Hint:** For feedback to be positive and growth-inspiring, it must be delivered properly, with enough attention paid to how the receiver will perceive and process it.

Diversity, Equity, and Inclusive Work Breakdown Structure (WBS)

An artifact to help guide the diversity, equity, and inclusion program and strategic plan to create an inclusive project environment is a work breakdown structure.

A work breakdown structure in project management breaks works into minor tasks or components to make the job more manageable and approachable.

Creating a Winning Team

Creating a winning team starts with staffing your project team with diverse and inclusive talent. The staffing management plan describes when and how employees will be acquired and how long they will be needed, including staff acquisition, training needs, recognition and rewards, and compliance.

> **PMO Nerd Checkpoint:** Organizational structure is a system used to define a hierarchy within an organization. It identifies each job, its function, and where it reports within the organization, including Lines of authority and roles and responsibilities.

Resource planning involves the strategic use of human and non-human resources to develop products and services under deadline and budget restraints. Resource meetings focus on sharing fact-based information and short-term planning for critical project activities and tasks. Resource Availability and Utilization is a planning technique to ensure that the project's allocated resources are available.

This is done by calculating the cost to use them, monitoring planned versus actual use of resources, and taking corrective action.

Resource Capacity Planning involves determining if the allocated resources are sufficient to complete new projects and determining if the number of resources, or the level of skilled people, is adequate on existing project teams. The resource management plan guides how company human resources should be defined, staffed, managed, and eventually released.

Team Development

The heart of the project is the project team. Team development is an essential part of creating a step to create an inclusive project environment. Team development includes forming, storming, norming, performing, and adjourning.

Forming

During the project's initiation phase, the team meets and learns about the project and its formal roles and responsibilities. Project managers are responsible for grounding rules, establishing "what success looks like," and developing team member assessments. Creating diversity, equity, and inclusion vision, mission, values, and goals as the team form is essential.

Storming

During the project's planning phase, the team begins to address the project work, technical decisions, and the project management approach. Project managers are responsible for communicating the "assumed norms" and understanding how people enter a conversation. One of the most critical steps in the storming phase is developing diversity, equity, and inclusion SWOT analysis and strategic plan.

Norming

Throughout the initiating, planning, and execution phase, the team begins to work together and adjust their work habits and behaviors to support the team. This is an excellent opportunity to reflect on the diversity, equity, and inclusion vision, mission statement, and goals. Verify and make sure Everyone's ideas have been heard as well.

Performing

During the execution phase, the project team reaches the performing stage function as a well-organized unit. Project managers are responsible for making sure everyone has a seat at the table, making sure everyone has an opportunity to speak, and value and respect everyone's opinion.

Adjourning

During the close-out phase of the project, the team completed the work and moved on from the project. Project managers are responsible for collecting and analyzing feedback on the project team's diversity, equity, and inclusion incentive.

> **PMO Nerd Recommendation:** Train staff to meet the new performance standards, make sure your team is cross-trained, set good performance targets for the staff, and identify leadership and organizational structure.

Team Alignment

Team development and team alignment go hand and hand. Team alignment is when all team members understand and support the project's shared vision and goals. During the initiating phase, we focus on collaboration to make it easier to get buy-in on the vision and objectives related to diversity, equity, and inclusion. Five influences on team alignment are culture, processes, information, planning tools, and barriers. Culture is the project team's attitudes, values, behavior, and environment. Execution processes are the project systems, processes, and procedures used to develop and deliver the project.

Information is the data elements, including business objectives, used to define the project's scope. Project planning tools are software programs, checklists, and aide-memoirs typically used to develop and manage projects. Barriers are obstacles to creating and maintaining the alignment of the project team.

> **PMO Nerd Checkpoint:** Vertical Alignment is a "Top-to-bottom" alignment between organizational stakeholders like executives, business managers, project managers, and functional specialists. Horizontal Alignment is a "Cross-organizational" alignment between functional groups within the organization, i.e., business, project management, and operations groups.

Team Building

Team building is a project-focused process that builds and develops shared goals, interdependence, trust and commitment, and accountability.

Chapter 4 Summary

This chapter focuses on a system approach to incorporate diversity, equity, and inclusion principles, tools, and techniques throughout the initiating and planning process groups. We unlock the methods to create a winning team by focusing on collaboration and team development. Vision, mission statement, values, and goals play an important role during the initiating phase. Creating a diversity, equity, and inclusion SWOT Analysis and Assessment, Strategic Plan. And Work Breakdown Structures (WBS) are tools to help create an inclusive project environment.

Key Topics:
- Vision, Mission Statement, Values, and Goals
- SWOT Analysis and Assessment
- Diversity, Equity, and Inclusion Strategic Plan
- Work Breakdown Structure (WBS)

5

Leading a Winning Team

"Equity in Project Management"

Chapter 5 Overview

This chapter focuses on a system approach to incorporate diversity, equity, and inclusion principles, tools, and techniques throughout the executing process groups. We emphasize the "Art of Project Management," including communication and conflict management skills required to lead an inclusive project environment.

Key Topics:
- The Art of Communication
- Active Listening Skills
- How People Enter Conversations
- Emotional and Conflict Management

Leading a winning team requires balancing the science and art of project management to meet the project requirements and achieve the project deliverables. Project managers are responsible and accountable for delivering the project on time and within budget; however, your team's welfare is also essential to success. This chapter will focus on the "Art of Project Management," i.e., the balance of people (project team), emotions, and conflict that can impact and influence the project indirectly.

Project Management Process Groups (Executing)

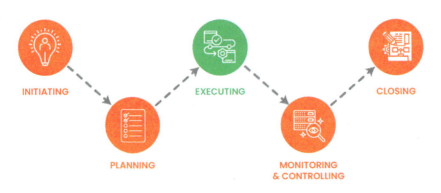

Figure 10.0_Project Management Process Groups

Executing Process Group

The purpose of the executing phase is to execute tasks, milestones, and deliverables for the customer, client, or project sponsor.

During this phase, project managers verify that the deliverables meet the project scope requirements and reaffirm the level of quality expected for the work being executed. Project managers manage and coordinate the resources available, review and manage risk, and make the necessary adjustments to meet the project requirements and deliverables.

> **PMO Nerd Checkpoint:** Some of the major activities include project teams carrying out their respective individual tasks, coordinating people resources, and managing stakeholders' expectations.

Project managers' roles and responsibilities for executing are:
- The Science and Art of Project Management
- Execution of Scope, Cost, and Schedule
- Quality Management
- Stakeholder Engagement and Management
- Executing the Project Deliverables

Leading a Winning Team

Leading the project team while balancing the customer, client, or project sponsor expectations can be challenging. As previously established, leading a team starts with self-reflection and understanding how your attitudes, beliefs, and behaviors can impact and influence the project team's performance.

The Art of Communication

The art of communication goes beyond conducting or supervising the exchange of information, and it includes the systematic planning, implementation, monitoring, and revision of all communication channels within a project. Communication is essential for leading an inclusive project environment because it can become the most significant barrier. There are many types of communication like verbal communication, nonverbal communication, written communication, and formal & informal. We are going to focus on nonverbal and informal communication. Nonverbal communication involves minimal use of the spoken language; gestures, facial expressions, and verbal fragments that communicate emotions without words; sometimes known as body language. For example, some people's facial expressions do not correctly reflect their tone or feelings. These differences can become communication barriers. When communication barriers arise in the workplace, it can be challenging to maintain and develop relationships with the project team.

> **PMO Nerd Hint:** Personality and social identity play a significant role in nonverbal communication. How you view your project team's nonverbal communication (positive or negative) is determined by identifying with each team member.

Every industry has its own set of unique words and phrases. While using these terms can seem more efficient sometimes, it's often confusing for those outside the field or with little or no professional experience. Some jargon can be offensive; therefore, consider the different meanings, and don't use words you don't understand.

Communication Styles

Understanding project team members' communication style is an essential step to removing any communication barriers.

There are three communication styles, aggressive, passive, and assertive. Each type may impact your project team communication based on your personality and social identity. Aggressive communication is described as expressing your feelings and opinions as they occur. Passive communication is carried out when the sender is not comfortable conveying his words, views, and even thoughts due to the fear of conflict. Assertive communication involves interacting in a way that respects both your rights and the rights of others.
Assertive communication often results in one's needs being met while also promoting respectful relationships.

For example, how does an aggressive communication style impact the project team? How does a passive communication style impact the project team? Remember, everyone has their unique communication style. Some people are outwardly expressive, while others maintain a more neutral tone.

> **PMO Nerd Checkpoint:** Project managers are responsible and accountable for communication management, including how your team interacts and engages.

Active Listening Skills

Active listening skills can help improve communication and reduce misunderstandings or lost information. Active listening is a process you can use to better focus on your conversation, understand and analyze data, and craft a thoughtful response. Recognize the employee using verbal affirmations to confirm your engagement in the conversation. Nonverbal communication can indicate how employees feel when they don't verbalize their feelings or reasons. You can reduce the challenge of identifying the problem by familiarizing yourself with nonverbal cues. You must communicate in various settings, whether online, in person, or over the phone, and through multiple channels, including email or instant messaging.

Techniques To Become an Active Listener

Active listeners will help project managers create an inclusive space where all team members feel valued, respected, and engaged. Techniques to become an active listener are:

- Paraphrase. Summarize the speaker's message's main point(s) to show you fully understand their meaning.
- Use short verbal affirmations. Short, positive statements will help the speaker feel more comfortable and show you're engaged and able to process the information they're providing.
- Display empathy. Make sure the speaker understands you're able to recognize their emotions and share their feelings.
- Recall previously shared information. Remember key concepts, ideas, or other critical points the speaker has shared with you in the past. This demonstrates that you're not only listening to what they're saying currently, but you're able to retain information and recall specific details.

Share Real Life Stories

Sharing real-life stories add a much-needed personal touch to diversity, equity, and inclusion, and encourage employees to open up and be empathetic. This is also an awesome way for your employees to get to know one another on a deeper level and appreciate each individual's experiences & perspective.

This activity is a great employee engagement idea as it encourages employees to share and actively listen to one another. Build empathy, strengthen workplace relationships, and learn more about your team by asking them questions. However, set some parameters around this activity so people don't feel forced to share or cornered into speaking about something they're not comfortable with.

How People Enter Conversations

Everyone enters conversations differently. As a project manager and leader, you are responsible for creating a safe and inclusive environment for everyone to communicate effectively and respectfully. Four common ways people enter conversation are thinking, acting, feeling, and believing. Thinking (Intellectual): Team members' primary response to issues or information may be a personal disconnect with the subject or a steadfast search for more information or data. Acting (Relational): Team members' primary response to issues or information actin or what is most often characterized as specific behaviors and actions. Feeling (Emotional): Team members' immediate response to problems or information through feelings, when it strikes them at a physical level and causes an internal sensation such as anger, sadness, joy, or embarrassment. Believing (Moral): Team members' primary response to issues or information from a deep-seated belief related to information or event.

Emotional and Conflict Management

Your capacity to comprehend your own emotions and how well you comprehend and react to the feelings of others are both indicators of your emotional intelligence. Being sympathetic and understanding of others is frequently a sign of emotional intelligence. Since emotional intelligence may enhance interpersonal skills, customer service, employee retention, morale, teamwork, and other areas, employers look for applicants who possess it. Conflict is inevitable in project teams involving more than one person. Project managers and team members must manage conflict effectively for successful project delivery. Five conflict strategies are:

- Avoiding (avoid the conflict and postpone the decision)
- Collaborating (try to meet the needs of all involved)
- Competing (take a firm stand and use positional power to conform to one perspective)
- Accommodating (giving in to others)
- Compromising (satisfy partially everyone)

Conflict resolution can be defined as the informal or formal process that two or more parties use to find a peaceful solution to their dispute. Several common cognitive and emotional traps, many of them unconscious, can exacerbate conflict and contribute to the need for conflict resolution.

Good Conflict vs Bad Conflict

Good Conflict	Bad Conflict
Produces New Ideas	Lowers Team Energy or Morale
Solves Continuous Problems	Reduces Productivity
Gives opportunity for People to Extend Skills	Prevents Job Accomplishment
Allows Creativity	Creates Destructive Behavior
Improves Performance	Fosters Poor Performance

Figure 11.0_ Good Conflict vs Bad Conflict

Personality and social identity play a significant role in how people enter conversations. How you view your project team (positive or negative) can impact your engagement and communication. How do you join discussions? (Thinking, Acting, Feeling, Believing) What are the pros and cons?

What is your conflict strategy? (Avoiding, Collaborating, Competing, Accommodating, Compromising) Which conflict strategy do you dislike the most? Does it impact how you engage and communicate?

Chapter 5 Summary

This chapter focuses on a system approach to incorporate diversity, equity, and inclusion principles, tools, and techniques throughout the group executing process. We unlock the keys to communication, active listening skills, and the importance of sharing real stories with your project team. We focus on understanding how people enter conversations and how each team member manages conflict.

Key Topics:
- The Art of Communication
- Active Listening Skills
- How People Enter Conversations
- Emotional and Conflict Management

6

Improving Team Performance

"Inclusion in Project Management"

Chapter 6 Overview

This chapter focus on a system approach to incorporate diversity, equity, and inclusion principles, tools, and techniques throughout the Monitoring, Controlling, and Closing process groups. We emphasize artifacts and tools to help project managers measure results against the initiation plan and adjust throughout the project life cycle.

Key Topics:
- Diversity, Equity, and Inclusion Evaluation
- Checkpoints and Surveys
- Metrics Reports and Dashboards
- Feedback, Lesson Learned, and Training

Developing and incorporating diversity, equity, and inclusion principles, tools, and techniques throughout the initiating, planning, and execution phase are essential in creating an inclusive project environment. Project managers are accountable and responsible for measuring and evaluating results; therefore, identifying, assessing, and evaluating diversity, equity, and inclusion strategies against the results is a critical step to measuring success. This chapter will focus on continuous improvement and team performance by incorporating data and metrics to measure diversity, equity, and inclusion throughout the project life cycle.

**Project Management Process Groups
(Monitoring & Controlling)**

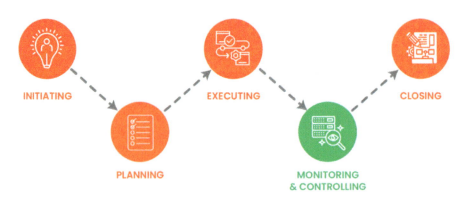

Figure 12.0_Project Management Process Groups

Monitoring and Controlling Process Group

In the monitoring and controlling process, project managers oversee all variations. A comparative analysis is carried out between what has been achieved against the baselines determined in the planning phase. When an affected area is recognized, the need and implementation of appropriate changes are evaluated urgently, preventing the entire project from being impacted. This process is leveraged to monitor and re-prioritize risks. After all, actions of nature, market factors, or even the progress of activities can cause changes that modify the order of risks. The project manager's role and responsibilities for monitoring and controlling are:

- Project Team Meetings & Reports
- Stakeholder Team Meetings & Reports
- Tracking Cost and Schedule Performance
- Integrated Change Control
- Managing Risk

Diversity, equity, and inclusion utilize the same methodology as monitoring and control. The first step to measuring your diversity, equity, and inclusion strategy's success is conducting an evaluation.

Diversity, Equity, and Inclusion Evaluation

Diversity, equity, and inclusion evaluation is a process for obtaining valid data and information about the performance of an organization on essential diversity, equity, and inclusion factors. As you plan for evaluation and assessment of your project diversity, equity, and inclusion efforts, determine critical collaborators and stakeholders who will help gather or provide feedback and data. Project managers must conduct ongoing evaluations throughout the project life cycle. Five diversity, equity, and inclusion evaluation methods are:

- Ranked method metrics are single statements where respondents answer on a scale of 1 to 5, one being a "strongly disagree," and five being a "strongly agree."
- Initiative-focused metrics are things you can easily track and are tied to progress on a numbers-based initiative.
- Demographic diversity, equity, and inclusion metrics should be measured carefully and not used as the sole marker of success in diversity, equity, and inclusion projects. Tracking these numbers is essential to identify areas that may have problems.
- Company-wide metrics help show the impact of diversity, equity, and inclusion projects on the business. They should be looked at in isolation and correlated to the available data through ranked method statements and demographic information.

- Correlational metrics are primary storytellers when measured against ranked method, demographic, and company-wide metrics.

Diversity, equity, and inclusion evaluation go beyond collecting and analyzing data. Pay attention to how social identities and personalities play out in your workgroup and organization. Consider which social identity groups do not often interact in your current work structure and how you might arrange opportunities for connection. Transparency is key. Communicate what they are doing and how they are doing it transparently so that others trust that you are being objective. Actions align with the diversity, equity, and inclusion strategic plan.

Diversity, Equity, and Inclusion Checkpoints
Project teams require constant iteration and refinement. Project managers must schedule checkpoints to track progress and ensure their diversity, equity, and inclusion initiatives lead to change.
- Schedule regular diversity, equity, and inclusion check-ins with project team members. Make sure project team members feel safe by utilizing a diversity, equity, and inclusion coach to conduct monthly or quarterly touchpoints.

- Analyze the diversity, equity, and inclusion strategy successes and failures with your project team. Refine diversity, equity, and inclusion strategy as needed.
- Surveys can be one of the best ways to connect with your team. Surveys are easy to customize, making them an excellent tool for measuring various aspects of inclusion and diversity.

PMO Nerd Hint: Project managers should collaborate with the project team and discuss if the unit is fulfilling the diversity, equity, and inclusion mission statement, vision, and goals. Discuss the ground rules and conflict; what's working? What's not working? Collaborate and refine as needed.

Diversity, Equity, and Inclusion Metrics Reports and Dashboards

Diversity, equity, and inclusion metrics will track and report on shifts up or down, trends, and other indicators representing progress and outcomes that enhance diversity, equity, and inclusion. There is no standard or universal metrics to measure diversity and inclusion. To measure qualitative metrics, you'll want to use an analytics or business intelligence platform with a custom dashboard that allows you to collect the relevant data and easily visualize it and extract actionable insights.

> **PMO Nerd Recommendation:** Host a monthly diversity, equity, and inclusion meeting and share the metrics reports and dashboards with the project team. Discuss the trends and allow everyone to provide inputs and voice concerns.

Project Management Process Groups (Closing)

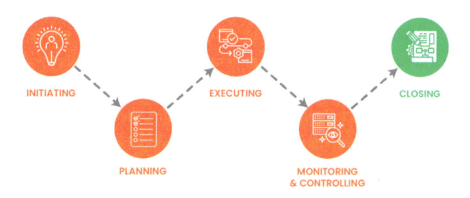

Figure 13.0_Project Management Process Groups

Closing Process Group

The closing process's purpose is to close the project or project phase formally. The project team has met the project requirements and achieved the project deliverables.

The critical point of this process is the customer, client, or project sponsor's acceptance of the product or service and signing off on the completion. The project Manager's Role and Responsibilities for closing are:

- Conduct a Walk-thru/Acceptance Meeting
- Create a Close Out Checklist
- Conduct a Closeout Meeting
- Closing Out the Project
- Lesson Learned

Throughout the initiation phase, you created a diversity, equity, and inclusion vision, mission statement, values, and goals to promote collaboration and make team commitment. You utilized a SWOT analysis to identify your project team's diversity, equity, and inclusion strengths and weakness. During the planning phase, you developed a diversity, equity, and inclusive strategic plan and work breakdown structure as a guide to incorporate diversity, equity, and inclusion. During the execution phase, you could practice techniques like active listening and managing how people enter conversations and handle conflict. Throughout this, you utilized tools like diversity, equity, inclusion evaluation, checkpoints, and reports to measure diversity, equity, and inclusion results. Let's discuss some essential tools and techniques you must complete before closing the project.

Feedback

Collecting employee opinions and 360 feedback is essential. Gather information from the prominent people working with or affected by the evaluated person. One person can have a limited and sometimes biased view, whereas many people should provide a more accurate and complete overview. Develop and implement a plan to give all managers access services to receive employee feedback and coaching for inclusion at work. The workplace becomes inclusive when more people collaborate and share their experiences while working on a project.

Additionally, it helps foster a sense of belonging among coworkers. We value cooperation and teamwork in the workplace because of this. Businesses must understand that running their organizations now must prioritize diversity, equity, and inclusion because of our times.

> **PMO Nerd Hint:** Ask your project team for input on how you might foster a more inclusive and open environment. You can implement a diversity policy thanks to their feedback. Your organization may have open discussions and adopt better practices thanks to these diversity and inclusion rules.

Post-Project Training

An essential element of improvement is training. Project managers should identify and promote the project team's training, education, and programming opportunities. Our experiences shape our views on diversity, equity, and inclusion in life, including socially, economically, and spiritly. As you close the project, create an action plan to help promote engagement and self-awareness, knowledge growth and learning, and workforce development. Racism/bias, intergroup dialogue, and professional skills are targeted to address behavioral, cultural, and systemic factors that activate discrimination and inequitable practices.

Chapter 6 Summary

This chapter focus on a system approach to incorporate diversity, equity, and inclusion principles, tools, and techniques throughout the Monitoring, Controlling, and Closing process groups. Diversity, equity, and inclusion evaluation go beyond collecting and analyzing data; project managers must balance real-life scenarios and adjust as needed to meet the project team's needs. The most critical aspect of closing the project is collecting project team feedback and developing a post-project strategy.

Key Topics:
- Diversity, Equity, and Inclusion Evaluation
- Checkpoints and Surveys
- Metrics Reports and Dashboards
- Feedback, Lesson Learned, and Training

Inclusive Leadership

Chapter 7 Overview

This chapter focus on the leadership skills required to be an inclusive and equitable project manager. We unlock the science and art of leadership, including the inclusive leadership principles, tools, and techniques needed to create an inclusive project team environment.

Key Topics:
- The Science and Art of Leadership
- Leadership Styles
- Social Perception and Attributions Influence on Leadership
- Inclusive Leadership Traits and Skills
- Inclusive Leadership Approach

Leadership in project management encompasses a wide range of duties, including efficient planning, project oversight, inspiring team members, and making critical decisions. Defining your leadership approach and understanding your roles and responsibilities are essential as a project manager. This chapter will focus on inclusive leadership principles, tools, and techniques to become an inclusive and equitable project manager.

The Science and Art of Leadership
Leadership is the influence, motivation, and inspiration of a group of people to act towards achieving a common goal. Leadership traits include change manager, facilitator, collaborator, diversity promoter, and humbleness.

Leadership core competencies include optimism, honesty, integrity, communication, organizational skills, and prioritization. Optimism refers to seeing things positively and expecting things to turn out well. The mood of the project manager can impact the project team, focusing on the positive and developing a plan to overcome any barriers. Honesty and integrity play an essential role in leading by example. Honesty refers to truthfulness and non-deception. A team leader with integrity is more likely to be trusted by their team members and will often be respected and appreciated by the team.

Communication is crucial when working with and leading a group because you must communicate with your team, leadership, and stakeholders. A team leader must communicate effectively and be directive. Strong organizational skills will help you monitor progress and keep team members motivated. Prioritization skills are essential competencies. Your capacity to focus on overarching objectives while giving attention to urgent short-term activities is also reflected in your ability to prioritize. Project managers are responsible for leading an inclusive project team that works closely with internal and external stakeholders to complete the project on time and within budget. Project managers who serve as a leader must balance management and leadership roles and responsibilities.

Management vs Leadership Roles and Responsibilities

Management Roles	Leadership Roles
Plan and Budget	Create Vision and Strategy
Organize and Staff	Maximize Opportunities
Direct and Control	Create Shared Culture and Values
Use Position Power	Use Position Influence
Culture of Efficiency	Culture of Agility and Integrity

Figure 14.0_ Management vs Leadership Roles and Responsibilities

PMO Nerd Hint: Your ability to manage your time effectively depends on establishing and maintaining an organized workstation. This could entail creating and implementing successful methods or learning how to use your resources most efficiently.

Leadership Styles

Project leadership is directing a team toward completing a project. The first mistake in trying to define leadership, though, is believing that it can be reduced to a single concept. You must be willing to think broadly and accept this because there are many different types of leaders worldwide, particularly in the more esoteric sector of project management. Regardless of your leadership style, leaders must incorporate moral leadership.

PMO Nerd Checkpoint: Moral leadership is about distinguishing right from wrong and doing right, seeking the just and the honest while achieving the goals and fulfilling purpose.

Common leadership styles are transformational, democratic, laissez-faire, transactional, autocratic, strategic, and charismatic. Transformational Leaders inspire their staff through effective communication and collaboration, thus initiating the path to success.

Democratic Leaders usually report higher levels of job satisfaction, and the company can benefit from individualistic creativity. Laissez-faire leaders are known for their hands-off approach, often criticized for poor role definition for managers. Transactional leaders are focused on group organization, establishing a transparent chain of command, and implementing a carrot-and-stick approach to management activities. Autocratic or authoritative leaders take control of the staff and rarely accept or consider employees' views or suggestions. The Strategic Leadership style involves a leader who is essentially the organization's highest authority. Strategic leaders are not, however, limited to the top management of the company. Bureaucratic leadership models are most suitable for highly regulated or administrative environments, where adherence to the rules and a defined hierarchy are essential. Charismatic Leadership is evident in both charismatic and transformational leadership. Both the leadership styles rely heavily on the cheerful charm and personality of the leader.

Social Perception and Attributions Influence on Leadership

Perceptions play a role in leadership because they can create an error in perceptual judgment that arises from perception inaccuracies. Perception is the process people use to make sense of their surroundings by selecting, organizing, and interpreting information.

As leaders, you must safeguard against the halo effect, developing an overall impression of a person or situation based on one characteristic, either favorable or unfavorable.

Inclusive Leadership Traits and Skills

Inclusive leadership traits and skills are adaptabilities, cooperation, creativity, and enthusiasm are essential in creating an inclusive project environment and culture. Adaptability skills are critical in inclusive leadership. Your capacity to process, manage, and react to changes is reflected in your adaptability. You must feel at ease in your ability to test out novel ideas or alternative approaches in the workplace. Flexibility helps you collaborate with others by allowing you to alter your initial project plan to suit their vision better. Cooperation skills are a leadership trait that refers to your capacity for teamwork. This is performing your unique activities or goals to help achieve a common purpose, which could need making concessions to other people and providing and accepting feedback. Cooperation abilities are crucial for working with consumers and help you prepare to face various circumstances. How well you collaborate with others on a project to accomplish a common goal is a measure of your collaboration skills. These abilities enable you to develop a team-first mindset that puts collective success before individual accomplishment.

Collaboration skills are highly crucial when you work in a team with people from different backgrounds and must adapt to varied situations or employ various communication methods. Creativity is a hiding skill that helps with becoming a change agent. You can approach problems in fresh ways by using your creative talents. With the help of these abilities, you can contemplate new ideas that question the existing quo while looking at all sides of an issue. Many employers value creativity because it frequently results in innovation that moves the business in new ways. Your enthusiasm for the profession or preferred industry is considered enthusiastic. Leaders must contribute and invest in the culture of the company and its expansion.

Inclusive Leadership Approach
Inclusive leadership calls for leaders to ensure all team members are treated fairly, feel valued and belong, and have the tools and assistance needed to realize their utmost potential. The inclusive leadership approach is the combination of three leadership styles, Empathetic Leadership, Servant Leadership, and Situational Leadership.

An empathetic leader is a leader with a working awareness of the nonverbal emotions another person may display.

A compassionate leader understands how to meet team members' emotional needs while promoting productivity and maintaining accountability. The benefits of an Empathetic Leader are:

- Creating higher employee retention rates and better talent acquisition
- Developing honest relationships and trust with team members
- Understanding how to maximize productivity levels and increase motivation through the consideration of employee habits and behaviors
- Meeting team goals and helping the company generate profit due to better productivity levels

Situational leadership is a leadership style in which a leader adapts their leadership style to suit the current work environment and needs of a team. The benefits of a Situational Leader are:

- It recognizes the need for flexibility.
- It creates a comfortable environment for workers.
- It takes different developmental phases into account.
- It increases the awareness of the leader.
- It helps a team be able to work better together.

Servant leadership is about serving others, expressing empathy, and empowering people to move toward the goal.

A servant leader shares power, puts the needs of the employees first, and helps people develop and perform as highly as possible. The benefits of a Servant Leader are:

- Decisions are based on the benefit of all
- It encourages empathy
- People grow in a servant leadership environment

Chapter 7 Summary

This chapter focus on the leadership skills required to be an inclusive and equitable project manager. We focus on the science and art of leadership, including core competencies and common leadership styles. You learned the inclusive leadership traits, skills, and approach to create an inclusive project team environment.

Key Topics:
- The Science and Art of Leadership
- Leadership Styles
- Social Perception and Attributions Influence on Leadership
- Inclusive Leadership Traits and Skills
- Inclusive Leadership Approach

Developing a Growth Mindset in Leadership

Chapter 8 Overview

This chapter will focus on developing a growth mindset as a leader by providing principles, tools, and techniques to help foster an equitable project team environment without barriers to opportunities, including creating an inclusive space where all team members feel welcomed, valued, respected, and engaged.

Key Topics:
- Emotional Intelligence
- Leadership of Tomorrow
- Establish a Culture That Respects Diversity
- Encourage Pay Equity
- Embrace Gender Pronouns

Leaders must display high emotional intelligence to foster an equitable project team environment without barriers to opportunities. Understanding emotional intelligence and developing a growth mindset will help leaders create an inclusive space where all team members feel welcomed, valued, respected, and engaged. Technical skills are required to manage projects effectively and produce the most outstanding results, but leaders must display high emotional intelligence and a growth mindset. This chapter will provide approaches to integrate diversity, equity, and inclusion into your leadership methodology and company's operations.

Emotional Intelligence

Emotional intelligence is the ability to perceive, identify, understand, and successfully manage your emotions and those of the people around you. People with high emotional intelligence know what they're feeling, what their emotions mean, and how these emotions can affect other people. For leaders, having emotional intelligence is essential for success. Leaders set the tone of their organization. It could have more far-reaching consequences if they lack emotional intelligence, resulting in lower employee engagement and a higher turnover rate.
While you might excel at your job technically, those technical skills will get overlooked if you can't effectively communicate with your team or collaborate with others.

The five critical elements of emotional intelligence are self-awareness, self-regulation, motivation, empathy, and social skills. As a leader, the more you manage each of these areas, the higher your emotional intelligence.

Leadership of Tomorrow

The organization's fundamental beliefs, company culture, and hiring procedure must change if workers are to be supported and a diverse workforce is to be achieved. It is insufficient for a business to discuss the current racism and systematic inequality problems without genuine efforts to combat them. It is critical to create inclusive systems and raise the bar above the minimal requirements for years without leading to any change. When it comes to workplace inclusion and diversity, it is time to take a proactive rather than a reactive approach. The only way to have an influence is to re-evaluate the underlying principles of businesses and the frameworks that direct their day-to-day operations.

The best method to implement diversity, equity, and inclusion on your project team and within your company is to garner support from leadership, peers, and the project team. Start the essential dialogues with the leadership. Then, spread the word about the initiative throughout your project team and company, and it can thereby become ingrained in the corporate culture.

Some approaches to integrating diversity, equity, and inclusion into your company's operations are listed below:
1. Establish A Culture That Respects Diversity
2. Conduct Diversity, Equity, and Inclusion Training
3. Host A Diversity, Equity, and Inclusion Focused Lunch and Learn
4. Play Diversity, Equity, and Inclusion Themed Games
5. Encourage Pay Equity
6. Think About Gender Pronouns
7. Support Diversity, Equity, and Inclusion Mission-Driven Brands

Establish a Culture That Respects Diversity

Every employee at our organization is aware of and cognizant of their place in our culture. All our staff members are urged to recognize, value, and utilize their differences to enhance their work. Incorporating all employees at all levels may create sustainable change because a top-down strategy does not inspire dedication.

Conduct Diversity, Equity, and Inclusion Training

A long-term dedication to diversity, equity, and inclusion is excellent for business, enhancing creativity, employee engagement and retention, customer happiness, brand reputation, and profitability, as successful firms know.

Although there isn't a single method, experts concur that a thorough approach is required to integrate diversity, equity, and inclusion into the corporate culture and the choices, policies, procedures, and practices that support it. An inclusive workplace where members of underrepresented or marginalized groups are encouraged to participate, contribute, lead, and thrive can be achieved with the help of behavior-based diversity training.

> **PMO Nerd Recommendation:** Host small, optional group sessions in the office led by a DEI professional. Encourage employees to share their unique stories within the group sessions. Group sessions are an opportunity to understand team members' experiences and collaborate with the DEI professionals to incorporate change to improve the work culture.

Host A Diversity, Equity, and Inclusion Focused Lunch and Learn

Lunch and learns are a great team-building activity for work because they provide your employees with an opportunity to collectively learn about an engaging topic. Hosting diversity, equity, and inclusion-focused lunch and learn events are a non-intimidating way for your employees to learn more about diversity, equity, and inclusion topics in a more relaxed setting.

Diversity, equity, and inclusion lunch and learns is a fun way to motivate employees to continue their diversity, equity, and inclusion learning journey.

> **PMO Nerd Hint:** Generate excitement around the event by sending out invite information well ahead of the event date. Partner with a local minority-owned restaurant to have food delivered to the office for your lunch and learn session.

Play Diversity, Equity, and Inclusion Themed Games
Whether looking to host an online group game, find the perfect icebreaker, or host an event in person, there are many diversity, equity, and inclusion themed games you can do with your team. diversity, equity, and inclusion games allow your team to learn, grow, and have fun all at once. Participating in diversity, equity, and inclusion games is a fun way to support employee engagement & learning while also creating a sense of belonging.

> **PMO Nerd Hint:** We recommend encouraging team members to participate in diversity, equity, and inclusion games, but not requiring them to do so. Everyone's comfort level varies depending on the activity and engagement tends to be higher when employees opt in.

> **PMO Nerd Recommendation:** Host a fun office activity like Step Apart, Step Together. In this game, two team members step apart when the team calls out something they have a difference and step together when they share a similarity. It's a great way to celebrate differences but shows that commonality exists as well.

Encourage Pay Equity

Managers must provide equal opportunities for all employees and level the playing field. Companies can use a variety of metrics to identify which individuals are being paid too little for jobs with comparable responsibilities. Managers may diligently aid in identifying any potential pay gaps between the team and the leaders by using people analytics. This method can examine trends within important departments to understand the underlying causes of such problems. This ground-breaking understanding will make it easier to identify trends and patterns in which a particular group of employees is underpaid within company sectors.

Embrace Gender Pronouns

Embracing the fact that people identify with different gender pronouns is one easy way to integrate diversity, equity, and inclusion into your business practice. This fosters a more accepting and inclusive workplace, particularly for the LGBTQ+ population, which is a minority group. The employer may also include the employee's gender pronouns in their employee IDs and their names.

Support Diversity, Equity, and Inclusion Mission-Driven Brands

Supporting brands with a diversity, equity, and inclusion focus is an easy way to begin implementing diversity, equity, and inclusion initiative at your company. Consider partnering with a black-founded brand or a corporate wellness company that compliments your diversity, equity, and inclusion efforts. This diversity, equity, and inclusion activity helps to uplift minority brands who may have been overlooked or are struggling to compete against larger, more established companies and fosters an inclusive workplace.

PMO Nerd Hint: Create a diversity and inclusion moment during a meeting by encouraging your team to share one of their favorite brands, companies, or products that are either minority-owned or pushing diversity, equity, and inclusion efforts forward in an impactful way.

Chapter 8 Summary

This chapter will focus on developing a growth mindset as a leader by providing principles, tools, and techniques to help foster an equitable project team environment without barriers to opportunities, including creating an inclusive space where all team members feel welcomed, valued, respected, and engaged. You developed some approaches to integrating diversity, equity, and inclusion into your company's operations like diversity, equity, and inclusion focused lunch and learn and diversity, equity, and inclusion themed games. Embracing gender pronouns and encouraging pay equity are essential steps to creating an inclusive project team environment.

Key Topics:
- Emotional Intelligence
- Leadership of Tomorrow
- Establish a Culture That Respects Diversity
- Encourage Pay Equity
- Embrace Gender Pronouns

About the Author

Quincy M. Wright, CCM, PMP
President of PMO Nerd LLC

Quincy M. Wright, CCM, PMP, is a world-renowned Project Management Professional (PMP) and Certified Construction Manager (CCM) with 15+ years of experience leading organizations and project teams in commercial and government sectors. Mr. Wright graduated from Texas A&M University-Commerce with a Master of Business Administration (MBA). He also earned a Bachelor of Science in Construction Management and an Applied Science in Architectural Engineering Technology from the University of Cincinnati. Mr. Wright is a subject matter expert in project management, including project due diligence, project planning, execution, and closeout. Mr. Wright's portfolio includes commercial, industrial, manufacturing, utility-scale transmission & distribution, grid modernization, renewable energy, and technology projects and programs. He is regularly sought after for speaking engagements, consulting, and coaching amongst organizations worldwide related to expertise in project management, agile, strategy, and creating inclusive cultures of belonging to enhance organization performance.

About PMO Nerd LLC

PMO Nerd is a professional training and coaching company. We provide highly interactive participant-driven coaching and training, engaging webinars, live world cafe-style workshops, and 24x7 on-demand learning.

Our mission is to guide and support individuals and companies throughout their project management journey by providing professional training and coaching services. Our goal is to help individuals and companies unlock the science and art of project management, including leading diverse and inclusive projects and project teams.

Our Services:
- Project Management Training & Coaching
- Construction Management Training & Coaching
- Proposal Management Training & Coaching
- Proposal Management Bootcamp
- Inclusive Leadership in Project Management
- 24x7 On-Demand Training
- Workshops and Webinars

Made in the USA
Las Vegas, NV
21 August 2022